Though It

Tarries

Though It Tarries

Tarries

Rev. Dr. Zen Miller

Williams and King Publishers

ISBN: 979-8-9897804-0-2

Printed in the USA, 2024

Dedication

This book is dedicated to my husband, Jerome, who came into my life as a precious gift from the Almighty God.

$\mathcal{F}$oreward

There is a wealth of literature in the area of spiritual encouragement and development, however, few of these books have dealt with the practical aspects of reassurance, transformation, and revival by the revelation of the Holy Spirit. I have had the privilege of knowing Dr. Zen Miller for more than 10 years and have seen the Lord Jesus Christ use her prophetically which has been manifested and authenticated in the way in which she writes and ministers to people of her church community.

This book *Though it Tarries* was given to Dr. Miller in a vision from God, thereby making it a volatile, explosive, and combustible weapon that, as children of God, we need during these times when there are great trials, tribulations, and warfare against the church of God.

Believers of Christ who have been fighting and are still fighting will come to understand that even when God is silent, He is there and working on their behalf. Thus, this book will resuscitate and reignite the flame that has gone cold. According to Jeremiah, Then I said, I will not make mention of Him, nor speak anymore in His name. But His Word was in my heart like a burning fire shut up in my bones: I was weary of holding back, and I could not, *(Jeremiah 20:9 NKJV)*. Therefore, when we get tired of the fight, this book encourages us to persevere.

I acknowledge with deep gratitude the influence that Dr. Miller has had in my ministry. She is a powerful inspirational speaker, and I would encourage every child of God to get a copy of this book because of the spiritual benefits to be gained. I would also urge pastors to do something special for others by buying several copies and giving to their members as gifts.

Dr. Joel White

This book is authentic and practical. Its contents cause you to identify with some of the characters. This book inspires you to step out in faith and hold on to your belief as you trust God to come through for you.

Keesha A. Phillps
(Daughter)

Greetings Readers,

I am coming to you on a personal note about this author, Dr. Zen Miller. I met Dr. Miller at a nursing home where I was employed as a nurse manager and from that day until today, I have nothing but respect for my second mother, pastor, teacher, and guide.

Dr. Miller always says, "All churches don't have the same ministry but they all should have one thing in common, which is soul winning". As of the writing of this book, it has been twenty-six years that I have thanked the Lord Jesus Christ for guiding me to Healing Waters Ministries.

Dr. Miller has been teaching me and guiding me since I was saved. As in *2 Timothy 3:16,* she has been using the scriptures to show our congregation love by reproof, correction and instruction. Twenty-three years ago, she performed my wedding ceremony. In 2012 my husband and I decided to move from the area but when we told our pastor what our decision was, she said, "You'll be back". To cut a long story short; we had such a horrible experience that we were back within one year.

Of all ministries I have been exposed to before and after I got saved, there is no other pastor in the world I would want to follow. My pastor, teacher and guide is one of a kind because she is blessed and highly favored. You may not be in close proximity to visit our hospital, but this book *Though it Tarries* will guide and help you to strengthen your walk with the Lord Jesus Christ. Soul Winning – that's what it's all about!

Doria E. Jumpp

Greetings.

I am an ordained minister with the Church of God, and the pastor of Faith Deliverance Worship Center in Kissimmee, Florida for the past five years. During this time, I have been honored to meet my pastoral colleague and friend, Dr. Zen Miller. Dr. Miller has been a pioneer of both spiritual development and a great resource to a community of people from all levels of society, who are searching for answers to their day-to-day challenges. What strikes me most about this Woman of God is her ability to connect with people and her willingness to help those who are feeling spiritually handicapped and hopeless in their lives. But most importantly, her own personal challenges and successes comprise the essence of who she is as a person.

Her book *Though it Tarries*, is a grand collection of self-help materials, which speaks to the inner man, and supplies the tools that will guide a soul through the process of waiting on God, and that can transform a crippled life, into a life of spiritual renewal and personal success! Within these pages, it is undoubtedly the foundation of the Holy Spirit's own work, which has never lost its power.

Dr. Zen, I look forward to the testimonies of each person who gets hold of this book, and I eagerly await your next best seller!!

Your colleague,
Pastor Beverly Gordon

I have known Dr. Zen Miller, my pastor and mentor for over 15 years. From the first time I met her, I discovered that she loves God. She is gifted in accurate prophecy, and always craves to be one with The Holy Spirit. She moves powerfully, allowing the Holy Spirit to use her mightily as the pastor for Healing Waters Ministries.

I am honored to endorse this book *Though it Tarries* as it will heighten your faith as you wait on God for His response to your situation or quest.

Deaconess Avril Lewin

This book entitled "Though it Tarries", which is written by my mother, Reverend Dr. Zenn A. Miller, will help people in both the Christian and Secular communities. Teaching them to trust God even when the answer or response is not in focus.

Alwayn Marie Grant
(Daughter)

Table of Contents

CHAPTER One

Even Though it Tarries

What is *it?*

It is your dream, vision, aspiration, promise, Word of Wisdom, Word of Prophecy that was spoken to you or over you. It is whatever you are waiting on or for, which has not yet been fulfilled.

The gestation period for a baby's development is approximately thirty-six weeks. As the pregnant mother waits, it is incumbent to prepare for the baby's arrival, even though the birthing seems so far away and without any evidence that this child could be born without complication.

It is not easy to wait on the Lord or anyone when you are going through trials, troubling or adverse situations, but wait on the Lord: be of good courage, and He shall strengthen thine heart: wait, I say, on the Lord *(Psalm 27:14).* The Lord is good unto them that wait for Him, to the soul that seeketh Him *(Lamentations 3:25).*

While you are waiting, do not lose focus. Just like a camera, what you focus on will develop. After Jesus' resurrection, He appeared to 500 of His disciples and told them to go to Jerusalem and wait there until they were endued with power from on high. However, on the Day of Pentecost, only 120 were present in the Upper Room waiting on the promise, the Holy Spirit. They experienced the powerful outpouring of the Holy Spirit, while 380 followed their own agenda and missed out on the promise. When we follow our agenda and refuse to wait on God, we find ourselves missing the mark as well as the blessing.

Even though you have been waiting on your promise and you still have not seen its manifestation, hang in there because God is a fixed Principle. He will show up. Be reminded that even Jesus Christ could not come to earth before His time. Even Mary had to wait on the right time of delivery as well. Imagine Mary and Joseph fleeing to Egypt because Herod the King sought to kill Jesus. Even though there was no room at the inn, that did not stop Jesus from being born at the right time. The scripture declares that when the fullness of time came, God sent forth His Son, made of a woman, made under the law, to redeem those under the law that we might receive the adoption as sons *(Galatians 4:4-5)*. Even though His parents had to flee to Egypt, and even though there was no availability at the inn, God so structured it that His parents found accommodation in the manger, with an on-time birth so that His purpose could be fulfilled. I would like to encourage all readers to continue to wait. Sometimes we may not understand why there are so many roadblocks in the direction that we are going, but each roadblock is preparing us so that we can fulfill our purpose as God ordained it.

Sometimes, when you are waiting on or for something, all hell seems to break loose in your life. Adverse situations begin to happen one after the next. This reminds me of an adage that says, "If not the button, then it's the buttonhole." This kills all enthusiasm to wait any longer, especially when the main thing you are waiting on is moving at a snail's pace. This is when there is nothing going for you and your faith begins to diminish.

I have a friend who had a vision about a product that she should invent. She thought that the gates of hell could not stop this product from selling, and nothing could abort her success because she was given this product in a vision. She did not realize that bringing item to market was a process. She became very angry, upset, and discouraged when she found out that she had to do a feasibility study to ascertain the need and market for the product. Then, she needed a sales pitch, a license, a patent, managers, producers, and lawyers. She thought it was not her responsibility to provide or help with any prerequisites or requirements to make this vision a reality. Before she could take her product to market, she did not realize the preparation, work, and investment that was required before she made her first dollar. We are like that sometimes. We want the results, but during the time of waiting, we do not think of preparing ourselves spiritually, mentally and emotionally for when we finally walk into our promise.

Uncertainty and lack of patience will cause you to try to rush God if He does not come through for you when you think He should, and how you think He should. I say God is a fixed Principle. Be patient. Paul said, "But if we hope for that we see not, then do we with patience wait for it," *(Romans 8:26)*.

Yes, it seems as if you have been waiting on the promise for years which seems like forever, with no reward in sight, but don't give up. Hold on a while longer. You might be giving up at the very moment that God decides to grant your request or fulfill your *it.* But do not grow weary in well doing because your labor will not be in vain, *John 9:10.* And let us not grow weary of doing good, for in due season we will reap if we do not give up *(Galatian 6:9).* Be reminded that there is a season for and a time for every purpose under heaven .

You may think that you are out of sight and out of mind, but not so with God. He is the All-Knowing God, and He will show up, show off, and show out.

I have heard concerted complaints from different people in the body of Christ as to why they should continue to wait on God for something that seems hopeless. But I must encourage you to continue to hold on because there is surety and security in the arms of Jesus, and He will never let you down.

I have had situations with impatience in my life, where my wrathful kettle was beyond its boiling point. I became 38 hot and was pistol ready to fire off my mouth because I had been waiting on my answer to many unfulfilled prophecies (my *it*). I needed time to chew and swallow what I had already been given. I fought hard to still trust, believe, and not throw the towel in. Whatever was promised to me, I needed it right away and because of impatience, I paid the price and lost out many times.

I urge you to continue to press on. Do not despise prophecy. Have faith in God. It won't be much longer. Continue to hold on to your belief until you receive from God His promise(s) that you have long-awaited.

It has been seen and heard among believers in churches all over the globe, that many have become impatient, bitter, upset, and weary because newcomers and new converts are so blessed. God has blessed them so much and those who have deemed themselves to be cornerstones and pillars of the church are still waiting for their answers, blessings and promises to manifest, even though they are faithful, die-hearted, and committed.

God's Word will remain God's Word. Don't walk away from the church, and don't stop waiting because payday is nearby. It is almost time for you to receive your award. The race is not given to the swift nor the strong but to he who endures until the end *(Ecclesiastes 9:11)*.

They that wait upon the Lord shall renew their strength, they shall mount up with wings as eagles. They shall run and not be weary; they shall walk and not faint *(Isaiah 40:31)*.

CHAPTER Two

Delay is not Denial

It has been seven and fifteen years, respectively, since I received several prophetic Words from the Lord, and I have yet to see the fulfillment of either of them, but I still believe and endorse the lyrics of the song entitled, "They are sure if you only believe; God's promises are sure."

There are times when promises are fulfilled in an instant. Then, there are promises that take a while to fulfill because they are given as Words of Wisdom and are for future happenings. Therefore, if God does not seem to be working as a catalyst to bring your promise to pass, continue to hang in there. But beloved, be not ignorant of this one thing, that one day with the Lord is as a thousand years, and a thousand years as one day *(II Peter 3:8)*. Our natural eyesight is limited, and, as a result, we see in part, but we serve a God who sits high and looks low *(Psalm 138:6)*. He sees the whole picture; therefore, we should trust Him to fulfill that which He has promised. The Lord is not slack concerning His promises, as some men count slackness; but is longsuffering towards us, not willing that any should perish, but that all should come to repentance *(II Peter 3:9)*.

If your promise does not come to pass in the time frame you thought it should, that does not mean that God has amnesia, and He has forgotten. God is not a man that He should lie, neither the Son of Man that He should repent: hath He said, and shall He not do it? Or hath He spoken, and shall He not make it good? *(Numbers 23:19)*. He has made a covenant with us. My covenant I will not break, nor alter the things that are gone out of my lips *(Psalm 89:34)*.

As you continue to wait on the Lord, Satan continues to check you out, as he did with Job. He is trying to determine your mindset but be reminded that he came with a threefold ministry—to steal, kill, and destroy. But Jesus said, I have come that you may have life and have it more abundantly *(John 10:10)*. God's Word is God's Word. It will come to pass.

We are instructed by the prophet Habakkuk that when we receive the vision, we should write it plainly upon tables that he may run with it who reads it. This vision is for an appointed time, but in the end, it shall speak and not lie. Though it tarries, wait for it, because it will surely come to pass.

God has set appointments for us, and we will continue to set appointments for ourselves throughout the course of our lives. Appointments are agreements to meet one or more individuals or groups at a certain date, time, and place. In our daily lives, we have appointments, whether it be medical, interviews, jobs, or otherwise. The days of our years are threescore years and ten (70); and if by reason of strength they be fourscore years (80), yet is their strength, labor, and sorrow; for it is soon cut off, and we fly away *(Psalm 90:10)*. As it is appointed unto men once to die but after this the judgment *(Hebrew 9:27)*.

It is still vivid in my mind today, as it was years ago when I was a child. I watched my dad as he dug up the dirt, made a mound, and planted some yams. I would imitate him and make a small mound and plant my yam, too. My dad knew it would take six months for the yams to reach maturation and ready to be harvested. However, I went to bed with great anticipation and expectation, that when I woke up the next morning, the yams would have finished developing. I watched for daybreak, and I was out in the field ready to harvest my crop, or so I thought. I had no concept of time, germination, or maturation. I recalled very well, my dad saying to me, "Baby, it is going to take a l-o-n-g time before that yam would be ready to harvest. It needs sunlight, water, and other things to mature." I was just too young to understand the process, and so I cried. As I grew older, I realized that all the tears that I cried could not shorten the process, so I had to wait.

Waiting is a process. Whatever you are waiting on, continue to wait because God is the Omniscient, All-knowing One. He knows all the "Q" words: where, when, why, and how. Trust Him! There are times when atrocities and adversities come into our lives as a catalyst to propel us into our destiny, by way of the Destiny' Ship. At times we think we are on board then God shows up with His plan for our lives. He shows the beginning and the end but never reveals what to expect or what we would encounter or endure in the middle. But as you follow on to know and learn, everything will unfold.

My life has been spared many times from accidents and incidents because there were obstructions that caused a delay.

There were times when I was late for work because of road construction which sometimes resulted in detours, but that did not prevent me from getting to work. I got to work late, but I was not denied my job. I was reprimanded for being late, but I was not denied my check on payday. There were reasons for those delays and detours, and sometimes God will delay our promise or cause detours to prepare, shield, and protect us from what could have been detrimental. Delay is not always a bad thing. It can instill fear; however, it can also increase patience and heighten our faith.

I remember ordering a product online. I received confirmation that the product had been shipped, and that I should receive the package at a projected date and time. I also received a tracking number. However, two days after the projected delivery date had passed, there was still no delivery. I tracked the package to find out what caused the delay. The next day, I received the package. This is proof that delay does not mean denial. Trust God even when you cannot trace Him. Trust Him when you don't understand, even when you cannot see your way out, and when you don't know what's next. There are numerous blessings, even unseen blessings because of waiting. Don't stop waiting on the Lord.

After Naomi had lost her husband, Elimelech, and her two sons, Mahlon and Chilion, she told her two daughters-in-law, Ruth and Orpah, to return to their people in Moab. "Go back to your family," she told them because she could not have any more children to give them husbands. She had passed the age of childbearing, and even if she could have children, then would they wait for her sons to grow up so that they could have them as their husbands?

The story continues that Orpah kissed Naomi and returned to her people, but Ruth remained with her mother-in-law. Naomi encouraged Ruth to leave as well, but Ruth decided she was in it for the long haul. She was going to be there with Naomi through thick and thin. And Ruth said, "Entreat me not to leave thee, or to return from following after thee, for whether thou goest, I will go and whither thou lodgest I will lodge. Thy people shall be my people, and thy God, my God. Where thou diest, will I die, and there will I be buried." If Ruth had not taken this stand, then, she would not have met her Boaz, who ultimately became a part of the lineage of our Messiah, Jesus Christ. Patience is a virtue, and delay is not denial. No matter what the circumstances are, God will come through for you. Wait, and give God the autonomy and authority over your life. He is the Author and Finisher of our faith and the only one who can see afar off.

At age 75, Abraham received a promise from God that he would have a son. Years had passed, and to Sarah, Abraham's wife, it seemed as if God took too long to fulfill His promise, so she decided to help Him. She encouraged her husband to have an affair with the maid, Hagar (the bondwoman), and that affair produced a son named Ishmael. Twenty-five years later, Sarah became pregnant and had a son named Isaac (the promised seed).

Like Sarah, we sometimes become impatient, but it is incumbent to stop looking at our present locale and start looking at what God is showing us and where destiny wants to take us. Because of impatience, Sarah had to take in Ishmael instead of waiting on Isaac. When God gives a Word, we need to wait on its manifestation regardless of how we feel or what we feel. God is God all by Himself, and He does not need our help. We need to cry out to Him as we continue to wait in faith. David said, "I waited patiently for the Lord; He inclined unto me and heard my cry," (*Psalm 40:1*).

When the Almighty God—the God who does not renege—gives a promise or a Word, He affixes His signature on it and seals the deal. Therefore, even though it tarries, let's wait for it. Hold on to your faith no matter the circumstance. Now faith is the substance of things hoped for and the evidence of things not seen *(Hebrew 11:1).*

Sometimes, when we are waiting on our answer, it is easy to lose the feeling in our faith, but we need to continue to keep our mind on the Lord and trust Him. Thou wilt keep him in perfect peace, whose mind is stayed on thee: because he trusteth in thee *(Isaiah 26:3).*

It is easy to lose your faith, or the feeling in your faith, especially when there is no manifestation to ignite your expectation but be determined to stand come hell or high water, volcano, storms, or tsunami. The manifestation might take longer than you expect, and sometimes you might feel it will never come to pass but wait for it. I have heard it being said concertedly by believers, "I have started for the end, and the end is not yet." Since the end is not yet, let us continue to hold on until we reach the finish line.

CHAPTER Three

Wait Some More

$\mathcal{I}$f it seems slow, wait for it, for at the end it shall speak, and not lie: though it tarry, wait for it; because it will surely come to pass *(Habakkuk 2: 3)*.

When a word or a promise has been spoken over your life, the manifestation or fulfillment may move at a snail's pace. Sometimes this is when you see a display of trials, adverse situations, and external forces, after which frustration sets in. This is when some people find themselves at sixes and sevens. The uncertainty of what is to come and how long it will take causes them to waver. Their patience is now at war with waiting but wait some more knowing this; that the trying of your faith worketh patience, but let patience have her perfect work, that ye may be perfect and entire, wanting nothing *(James 1:3-4)*.

A young man named George Eastman yearned for the day when photography would be made available and accessible to the public. He wanted to be up-to-date and current with information pertaining to his desires and aspirations. He became interested in books and magazines related to photography and publications of foreign literature, namely, Spanish, French, and German. In the year 1881, George started his own business with dry plates, a product he developed. Business did not go well for him, so he had to refund money to all his customers that bought this product. Because he wanted to produce marketable products, George went back to the drawing board (his laboratory), where he began to experiment. In totality, he conducted 471 experiments. During this time, he invented an emulsion that was used to replace the dry plates. He also pioneered other products, such as the tripod and invented roll film. In the year 1895, eighteen years later, photography became available and accessible to everyone. Britanica.com/George Eastman.[1]

Before George's dream of popularizing photography came to life, his experiments had failed 471 times; however, this did not derail his vision, mission, or determination to succeed. Instead, it motivated him to persevere, and as a result, his pursuit brought about what was known as The Eastman Kodak Company.

There are times when waiting on God or anyone seems like a waste of time but let us continue to wait. I have heard it said many times that whatever is worth having is worth waiting for. If we continue to wait in expectancy, we will be rewarded.

We have heard, and we have read that the Lord is coming back. As we continue to wait for His return, let us work to be rewarded. *And behold I come quickly; and my reward will be with me, to give every man according as his work shall be (Revelation 22: 12).*

As you wait, do not murmur, or sit idly doing nothing, but continue to read, pray, and fast. *Continue to ask, and it shall be given unto you; seek and ye shall find; knock and it shall be opened unto you: for everyone that asketh receiveth; and ye that seeketh findeth; and to him that knocketh it shall be opened (Matthew 7:7-8).* Knocking is the superlative, third, and utmost degree. When the Holy Spirit constantly prompts you to knock, He is saying to you, "Wait some more. Hang in there a little while longer."

17

Jesus wants us to keep asking, keep seeking, and keep knocking until someone answers the door. God will not let us down and neither will He allow our enemies to triumph over us. God's Word is God's Word, and it will not return unto Him void. It will accomplish what it sent forth to do. That is what faith is, holding on to your belief until you receive, from God, what you have been waiting for. If you have not yet received your "it", wait some more.

If George Eastman had given up after his experiments failed 471 times, there would not have been an Eastman Kodak Company. I am reminded of a poem I learned in school at a very young age. It was William Hickson's 1845 poem *"Try Again"*, states, *'Tis a lesson you should heed, try, try, again. If at first you don't succeed, try, try, again.* [2]

Chapter Four

Be Tenacious, Hold On

Sometimes, other people's views or thoughts of us can influence our decision-making ability or destiny. There will always be opposition in life. No one is exempt. Satan will always try to sway or deter us, but with perfect submission to God, he will flee. Submit yourself therefore to God. Resist the devil, and he will flee from you *(James 4:7)*.

One day, a well-known man of authority, caliber, and status went to ask Jesus to heal his sick daughter. He was faced with many obstructions and much opposition that could have daunted or aborted his pursuit. But he was tenacious as a bulldog, and he was determined to win.

As you read the story of Jairus' daughter, you will be able to identify the obstructions that Jairus experienced:

1. He was opposed to fear. He did not want to lose his daughter, whom he loved.
2. He was opposed by tradition. He was a ruler of the Jews, yet he fell down and worshipped Jesus, which was not customary.
3. He was opposed by the attitude of the crowd. Anywhere Jesus went, there was always a crowd. Some people just wanted to see what was happening and some people wanted to be a part of what was happening.
4. While Jairus was still waiting on Jesus, he got the news that the woman who had an issue of blood for twelve years, had received her healing. This must have been devastating for him as he continued to wait on Jesus to come to his house.
5. He was opposed with doubt and unbelief among the people.
6. He was opposed to the people's emotions. They wept and grieved the passing of Jarius' daughter, but Jesus said, "Weep not, she is not dead, but sleepeth."
7. Jairus was mocked and criticized, but despite the mockery and criticism, he pressed through in faith because he knew that there was a blessing in the pressing. Come hell or high water, he needed healing for his daughter.

It is not hard for one's faith to fail after you have been faced with or have endured so many oppositions, but Jairus' faith stood the test of time. Many times, our faith is greater than our perception, but be tenacious and hold on.

Acts Chapter 27 states that Paul and certain other prisoners were determined to sail to Italy, but they were met with outrageous, boisterous, and contrary winds after they had sailed over the Sea of Alicia and got to the city of Lycia. The centurion found a ship of Alexandria sailing into Italy and put them on board. In the process, they were shipwrecked but not harmed. However, Paul was forewarned by an angel saying, "Fear not, Paul. Thou must be brought before Caesar. God hath given thee all those that sail with thee."

As they sailed, things got worse, and Paul told them that he perceived their voyage would be with hurt and much damage, not only to the ship and cargo but also to their lives. The centurion did not believe Paul, and as the south wind blew softly, they thought everything was fine, so they lifted the anchor. Not long after they lifted the anchor, a tempestuous wind Euroclydon beat against the ship with great force. The scripture declares that no one had listened to Paul. They were admonished by Paul for not heeding his words. However, he later encouraged them that there would be no loss of life, but the ship would be lost.

Unbelief can cause you to make foolish and rash decisions. Let me encourage you that while you are waiting on the fulfillment of your promise, storms and all kinds of adverse situations may arise. But hold on because the devil might slow you down, but he cannot kill you until your purpose is fulfilled.

While we are waiting on our promise, we should be all ears, and refuse to be unfocused. We should keep our minds stayed on Him. Doing so will help us to realize when our answers come.

Paul told his men about his angelic encounter and the message he received. He knew and held on to what the angel had told him. Even when God's will oppose your desires, continue to trust Him because you know what He told you. Be confident, be tenacious. Whenever God gives you a Word, the devil, his emissaries, and all of hell's occupants cannot prevent it from coming to pass. Do not let opposition instill fear in you. Wait for your change to take place. Is there not an appointed time to man upon earth? *(Job 7:1)*. All the days of my appointed time will I wait till my change come *(Job 14:14)*.

CHAPTER Five

Fear, the Thief of Time

Fear is false evidence appearing real. It has no substance or truth. It is a feeling induced by danger or threat. It is the thief of time, and the power that Satan utilizes to cripple and paralyze the people of God. The children of God should not have to develop a phobia because of Satan's plot or ploy. For God hath not given us the spirit of fear, but of power, and love and of a sound mind *(2 Tim 1:7)*.

Do not let fear intimidate you or cause you to miss out on what God promised you or what He has for you. He knows your destiny, and He is the Author and Finisher of your faith *(Hebrews 12:2)*. God told Jeremiah, "Before I formed you in the womb, I knew and approved of you (consecrated you). Before you were born, I separated and appointed you as a

23

prophet to the nation," *(Jeremiah 1:5)*. God also knew David and because David knew him, he said, "O Lord, thou hast searched me and known me. Thou knowest my downsitting and mine uprising; thou understandest my thoughts afar off. Thou compassest my path and my lying down and art acquainted with all my ways," *(Psalm 139: 1-3)*.

God is very true to his Word. He will not renege. My covenant will I not break, nor alter the thing that is gone out of lips. Once have I sworn by my holiness that I will not lie unto David *(Psalm 89:34-35)*. God's promises or Word will come to pass despite Satan's cunningness. Do not fear, but continue to pray, and believe and wait.

Jesus told Peter and the other disciples to get in the boat in order to go over to the other side. While they were in the middle of the sea, there arose a storm. Jesus was asleep in the bottom of the boat when fear got a hold of the disciples. Their faith became weak, and they went and woke Him up. The disciples questioned Him, "Don't you care if we perish? How could you lay there sleeping when the waves and the billows are raging out in the angry deep?" Fear was in opposition to their faith. Jesus arose and questioned them about their faith. He then spoke to the wind, and in obedience to His voice, the sea became calm as it was before the storm.

Regardless of where we are or how long we have waited for our answer or promise, we must always know that God will keep His Word. He will not turn His ear or His back on us. When Satan, who is our enemy, tries to instill fear in us to weaken our faith, be reminded that the Word of God declares that when the enemy shall come in like a flood, the Spirit of the Lord shall raise a standard against him *(Isaiah 59:19)*.

Do not allow fear to cause you to give up before you receive the answer to your prayers. Let faith be your fulcrum, (your stability). Let faith be your Shechem (shoulder to lean on), because without faith it is impossible to please Him, for he that cometh to God must believe that He is, that He is a rewarder to them that diligently seek him *(Hebrews 11:6)*.

Jesus said, "Simon, Simon, Satan, desires to sift you as wheat, but I have prayed for you, that thy faith fail not," *(Luke 22: 31-32)*. Satan wants to you to fail. It does not matter how spiritual you are, you can falter or become weak in faith.

Abraham, at one time, lost the feeling in his faith. As he was about to enter Egypt, he said to his wife Sarah, "I know that thou art a beautiful woman. When the Egyptians see you, they will say this is his wife, then they will kill me but let you live," *(Genesis 12:11)*. "Say that you are my sister, then everything will be alright for me, and because of you I will live," *(Genesis 12:12)*.

Elijah, the prophet, performed many miracles. He called down fire from heaven on Mount Carmel, and it consumed the sacrifice and killed 450 of Baal's false prophets *(1 Kings 18:17)*. Yet not long afterward, he was hiding from Jezebel, the queen who sought to kill him *(1 Kings 19:1-4)*.

The psalmist, David, a man after God's own heart, said during one of his tests, "What time I am afraid I will trust in thee?" *(Psalm 56: 3)*. Fear cannot avert God's plan for your life.

As Jesus was being seized and arrested in the Garden of Gethsemane, Peter drew his sword and cut off the right ear of Malchus, a servant of the high priest. Yet, not long afterward, he denied the same Christ who he had just previously identified as he declared, "Thou art the Christ, the Son of the Living God," *(Matt 16:16)*. Peter was fearful of death. When a person becomes a Christian, the devil does not send him or her on vacation, nor does he take one. He realizes that he has already lost one of his soldiers and will try his very best to recruit you and get you back into his army. He and his emissaries will instill fear in you. He will roar like a lion, but you know who the Conquering Lion of the Tribe of Judah is! Do not cringe. Be vigilant.

Fear has no boundary. It knows no color or race. Fear does not regard ethnicity, culture, or religion. Fear will present itself in any setting, at any time. They were on the way up to Jerusalem with Jesus leading the way, and the disciples were astonished, while those who followed were afraid *(Mark 10:32)*.

Another example of someone who had lost the feeling in his faith is Zacharias, the priest who visited the temple regularly to offer burnt offerings unto the Lord. One day, the angel Gabriel appeared unto him saying, "Fear not Zacharias for thy prayer is heard, your wife Elizabeth shalt bear a son who shall be named John." He questioned the angel saying, "Whereby shall I know this, for I am an old man, and my wife Elizabeth is well stricken in years," *(Luke 1:18)*. The promise of a son to Zacharias at this age seemed overwhelming and unreal so he doubted. Fear overtook him, and his faith began to wither. The angel identified himself to Zacharias and said, "I am Gabriel who stands in the presence of God, but I am sent as a messenger unto thee to speak to thee." Gabriel told him, "Behold thou shalt be dumb and not able to speak, until the day that these things be performed because thou believest not my words which shall come to pass in the season. And blessed is she who believed for there shall be a performance of those things which were told to her from the Lord," *(Luke 1:45)*.

When the Almighty GOD, the God who does not renege, gives a Word or a promise, he affixes His signature on it and seals the deal. Therefore, even though it tarries, let us wait for it. The Lord is not slack concerning his promise, as some men count slackness, but is longsuffering toward us, not willing that any should perish *(2 Peter 3:9)*. Hold on to your now faith no matter what. Now faith is the substance of things hoped for and the evidence of things not seen *(Hebrews 11:1)*. Determination and faith are vehicles that will take you to your destination. Fear not.

CHAPTER Six

Rejection, the Catalyst

Rejection is a feeling of being isolated or abandoned. It is the result of a refusal to accept, use, or acknowledge a person or idea by simply excluding him or her from a group or project. It can act as a catalyst to end or continue something that is to be. Rejection is very powerful to one's psyche. It can dampen or kill your spirit and aspiration, which in turn, causes you to give up.

Theodor Geisel was an American author, illustrator, political cartoonist, poet, and artist. He drew cartoons to be used in advertisements for an insecticide company named Flit. After some time, he desired to take on commercial advertisements, which did not work out for him, so he ventured into writing children's books, and again, things did not work out.

He sought a publisher for his first manuscript which he entitled, "A Story No One Can Beat." Based on his varied account, his book was rejected by 20-29 publishers. Due to the numerous rejections, he became frustrated and was ready to throw in the towel. One day, while he was walking down Madison Avenue in New York, he contemplated throwing away the manuscript when he got home. It so happened that he met one of his former schoolmates, Mike McClintock, who had just been appointed juvenile editor of Vanguard Press. McClintock promptly took him up to his office where they signed a publishing contract. This reunion was instrumental in the publication of Theodor's first book in 1937. He changed the title of his manuscript to "And to Think That I Saw It on Mulberry Street." He wrote four more books before he received the US honorary degree and before the United States entered World War II. He then had another chance to encounter Dr. Seuss. [3]

Theodor wrote over sixty books, and his work included several of the most popular children's books of all time, selling over 600 million copies that were translated into 20 languages by the time of his death. He was best known for authoring popular children's books under the pen name, Dr. Seuss. He was awarded the Pulitzer Prize in 1984, and in addition, eight honorary degrees. At the time of his death in 1991, at the age of 87, his books had sold 200 million copies. In 1993, two years after his death, two additional books were published based on his sketches and notes.

In 2000, Publishers Weekly completed a list of the best-selling children's books of all time. Of the 100 top hardcover books, 16 were written by Geisel which included, Green Eggs and Ham at number 1, The Cat in The Hat at number 9, and One Fish Two Fish, Red Fish Blue Fish at number 13.[4] With the countless rejects Theodor was faced with, he could have given up, but he held on for the long haul. Had he quit when his first manuscript was denied, or after almost 30 refusals from publishers, this story might not have been told.

When a person is overwhelmed by rejections, it takes steadfast persistence to continue or make it to the finish line. For example, if you're writing a book, a publisher may reject your manuscript, however, that does not mean it will never be published. Keep persisting until God opens the door for you. Theodor Geisel put it this way, "That's one of the reasons I don't believe in luck."[4b] I believe in receiving a blessing." A child of God does not believe in luck but in faith in the Son of God.

Even Jesus was faced with rejection; he knew how it felt to be denied. He came unto His own and His own received Him not, but as many as received Him to them gave He gave power to become the Sons of God *(John 1:1)*. He was despised and rejected of men; a man of sorrows and acquainted with grief: and we hid as it were our faces from Him, he was despised, and we esteemed Him not *(Isaiah 53:3)*. To whom coming, as unto a living stone, disallowed indeed of men, but chosen of God and precious *(1 Peter 2:4)*. Wherefore also it is contained in the scripture, Behold, I lay in Zion a Chief Corner Stone, elect precious: and he that believeth on Him shall not be confounded *(1 Peter 2:6)*.

Some people did not see Him for who he was declared to be. They called him Beelzebub, Joseph, the Carpenter's Son, and the devil. Nathanael said to Him, "Can anything good come out of Nazareth?" *(John 1:46)*. But Jesus did not let people's opinions of Him affect His determination to fulfill His purpose. When we have been rejected, it does not convey the greatest of feelings, but dare to defy people's adverse label that they have placed on us. See yourself through God's eyes. Accept yourself and heighten your self-esteem.

The apostle Paul had been rejected many times, which is why he was able to declare, "Brethren, I count not myself to have apprehended: but this one thing I do, forgetting those things which are behind, and reaching forth unto those things which are before. I press towards the mark of the price of the high calling of God in Christ Jesus," *(Philippians 3:13-14)*.

When adverse situations come, press on. When you feel alone like an island, don't be discouraged. One writer penned it this way, "God's right there with you. You may not see Him, but you're not alone. You're hurting now, but your morning is coming." Weeping may endure for a night, but joy comes in the morning *(Psalm 30:5)*.

Joseph was another person who also experienced rejection. He was thrown into a pit by his brothers, but despite all the fear, pain, subjugation, and subservience he encountered, he transitioned from the pit to Potiphar's House, from prison, and then to the palace. While he was in the pit, he could not see the palace. Sometimes we cannot see the reason we are placed in certain situations. Therefore, we ask the question, why me? Sometimes the revelation or answer lingers, but there will be an answer, and the rationale will be realized. We need to thank God for the bakers, and butlers that He has sent our way as we are walking through our valleys or trying to creep out of our pits. Like Joseph, you might have been placed in a pit, but it does not end there. Just know today that God is real, and He never fails. He said it, and He will do it. Do not allow people to control your destiny. When God shows up—and He will—everything will change. Continue to trust Him.

Jephthah, the illegitimate son of Gilead also knew about rejection. He was despised by his father's legitimate sons (his brothers) who excluded him from his family's inheritance. They cast out Jephthah, who fled to the land of Tob, a very desolate area in Syria where he formed a group, and they raided the surrounding territories. The elders of the Gilead region saw that he was cast out and they did nothing. However, during the Ammonites' invasion of Gilead, tribal elders sought his help because they saw that he was fearless. And they said unto Jephthah, come, and be our captain that we may fight with the Ammonites. And Jephthah said unto the elders of Gilead, did not ye hate me and expel me out of my father's house? And why are come unto me now when ye are in distress? *(Judges 11:6-7).*

And the elders of Gilead said unto Jephthah, therefore we turn now, that thou mayest go with us, and fight the children of Ammon. And Jephthah said unto the elders of Gilead, if ye bring me home again to fight the children of Ammon and the Lord delivered them before me, shall I be your head? And the elders of Gilead said unto Jephthah, the Lord be a witness between us if we do not so according to thy words *(Judges 11:8-10)*. Then Jephthah went with the elders of Gilead, and the people made him head and captain over them: and Jephthah uttered all his words before the Lord in Mizpah *(Judges 11:11)*. Jephthah could have chosen not to help the elders because they denied and treated him poorly, especially since they did not defend him. He could have chosen to get even with them.

When a person has been submerged in rejection, it takes a fixed purpose not to get even. But ye have heard that it has been said, an eye for an eye, and a tooth for a tooth: But I say unto you, that ye resist not evil: but whosoever shall smite thee on the right cheek, turn to him the other also *(Matt 5: 38-39)*. Do not be overcome by evil but overcome evil with good *(Romans 12:21)*. Let God be the judge. Be reminded that Jesus was the stone the builders rejected, but He became the Chief Corner Stone. Jephthah was rejected by the elders but later became their captain. Rejection can be a catalyst or an inhibition. Do your assessment as you continue to trust and wait on God.

Chapter Seven

It is Never too Late

Many elderly people have used their age as a deterrent and excuse for their unachieved goals or unreached destiny. This should never happen because a person's desire does not die because he or she is elderly. Not all elderly individuals suffer from cognitive impairment or decline; therefore, go after your aspirations. Your desire is to achieve something.

Over the years, I have seen numerous elderly people receive their high school diplomas and college degrees because, to them, it was never too late. The race is not to the swift, neither the battle to the strong, but those who endured to the end *(Ecclesiastes 9:11)*. Just take the first step, get on your mark. Get set. Then go! Age should not stop anyone from seeing or reaching the finish line. It is your perception.

Go after your goal. Go back to school and take one subject or course at a time. Pursue and excel. Do not look at the four years or length of time required to get your degree. Keep the big picture of graduation in the forefront of your mind. You are never too old to go back to school. Technology will also allow you to realize your dream by taking many courses from home on your computer, tablet, or an iPad. It's never too late to wear the cap and gown. *Hebrews 12:11* tells us that God is no respecter of persons. What He has done for one, He can and will do for all. If you desire to pursue Him, He will pursue you, so go after Him and after your goals.

When your mind is swarmed with indecisiveness and discouragement, it will cause you to abandon your vision and mission. But call on the name of Jesus, and He will answer you and show you great and mighty things that you do not yet know or see *(Jeremiah 33:3)*. In all thy ways acknowledge Him, and He will direct thy paths *(Proverbs 3:6)*. As you go day by day, God will see you through. Trust Him because it's never too late.

The world is filled with vision, however, it is also filled with dream-takers and dream killers. Sometimes, they are your friends, family, acquaintances, co-workers, as well as church folks who call themselves the people of God. Listen, do not allow anyone from these groups to speak negative words in your ears. Let your faith roll away the stones of doubt and intimidation. Remember that faith comes by hearing, and hearing by the Word of God *(Romans 10:17)*. Faith will replace doubt and put you in the overcomers and winner's circle.

Even though you have not yet attained what you are waiting on, and at times you feel weary because things seem to take too long, hold on to your belief until you receive your promise from God. Continue to glorify Him, give Him glory and praise, and be determined, devoted, and courageous. There was a time when David was faced with a very trying situation. He was greatly distressed, and he encouraged himself in the Lord *(1 Samuel 30:5)*.

As I mentioned previously—and it is worth reflecting once again—Abraham received the promise from God when he was seventy-five years old, but he allowed negativity, impatience, and the request of his wife, Sarah, to cause him to disobey God. He honored Sarah's request and slept with

Hager, the maid, and this affair produced Ishmael. Twenty-five years later, Sarah conceived, and the promise was fulfilled as Isaac, the promised seed, was born. It is never too late to see the manifestation of the Sovereign God.

When Simeon was old, and his eyes were dim, he waited for the fulfillment of the promised Messiah before his death and his soul departed. Simeon took Him in his arms and praised God saying, "Sovereign Lord, as you have promised, you may now dismiss your servant in peace. For my eyes have seen your salvation, which you have prepared in the sight of all nations: a light for revelation to the Gentiles, and the glory of your people Israel," *(Luke 2:28- 32)*. It is never too late for God to do what He said He is going to do. When you are at your Red Sea, God will show up because what is impossible with man is possible with Him. Be steadfast and unmovable. Do not lose your focus even though you are being ridiculed, laughed at, or jeered. Because when your enemy sees you as a failure, you will hear your spirit saying, "Success is mine. I can do all things through Christ who strengthens me," *(Phil 4:13)*.

You may stumble or drop out along your journey. You may drop out of school, your computer may mess up, or you may be unable to pay your tuition for a semester or two, but do not lose hope. One writer penned it this way, *"If you stumble and fall, my brother, if you stumble and fall, my friend, pick yourself up, brush yourself off, and start all over again.* [5] God is right there with you. You may not feel Him, but you are not alone.

You might be feeling down in your spirit but remember that weeping may endure for a night, but joy comes in the morning *(Psalm 30:5)*. Your answer is never too late, and neither is He.

Press toward your goal because your victory is ahead. According to *Hebrews 12:1*, therefore, since we are surrounded by so great a cloud of witnesses, who by faith have testified to the truth of God's faithfulness, stripping off every unnecessary weight and the sin which so easily and cleverly entangles us. Let us run with endurance and active persistence, the race that is set before us.

There is a very bright light at the end of the tunnel. Your gown is in place, you are outfitted, and your name has been called. Go ahead and walk across the stage. It is never too late.

CHAPTER Eight

Waited, Waited... and Still Waiting

Have you ever had this experience, or are you currently experiencing this situation? What situation? Waited and still waiting on something that you believed you should have already received. If your answer is yes, welcome to the club. This is where I have been hanging out for a couple of years.

Now come, let us reason together. What do you think, and how do you feel? Let me to be the first to say how I feel. I feel like giving up my membership with this dead-end club because I am tired of waiting. I am frustrated. Did you know frustration can cramp and paralyze your vision, mission, and ideas? Listen, whatever you have been waiting for, do not allow frustration to put a monkey wrench in your wheel. In other words, do not allow frustration to cause you to stop or to give up. Some signs of frustration are: anger, loss of self-esteem and self-confidence, depression, stress, losing your temper, feeling sad and anxious, irregular eating habits, trouble sleeping, turning to drugs and alcohol.

There can be negative as well as positive sides to frustration. It can put you in a very low and uncomfortable place, especially when you desire to eat at the king's table. This is like a Mephibosheth and David situation in the Bible. Sometimes, frustration can act as a catalyst to push you out of that low, dark place, and soon after, something else arises, and you realize that you still must wait. It can be so discouraging. Whatever happens, continue to wait, and just know that God is on the throne. He will remember His own, and He will not let you down.

We all need to learn to cope with our frustration to avoid taking it out on others. You are not alone, so whatever frustrates you, be reminded that there are others with the same issues and greater, but Jehovah Shammah (the one who is always present) is always right there. God is a very present help in times of trouble. Therefore, do not panic even though the earth be removed and though the mountains are carried into the midst of the sea, and there seems to be no end in sight to your waiting. Know that God did not bring you this far to leave you, and He gave His Word, "I will never leave you nor forsake you".

Frustration can bring about uncertainty. It can play tricks with your mind and feelings, but as you muse, you will realize that a metamorphosis is taking place and character is being built amidst all that is going on.

Yes, there is good news! You can overcome frustration and win this battle. Do not lie to yourself by saying, "I am not frustrated." Go ahead and acknowledge that you are frustrated. Continue to praise and thank God despite how you feel. Put your trust in Him even when things seem hopeless, and your vision is not coming to pass. Even though you are frustrated, lift your eyes unto the hills from whence cometh your help. Stay focused because the very God of Abraham, Isaac, and Jacob wants you to have a successful end concerning His plans and thoughts for you.

As you wait on the Lord for your positive outcomes, thorns and prickles may spring up in your way to slow you down. But despite all these thorns, God's grace is sufficient for you, and He will see you through. Your dream will not die. Joseph, the dreamer, encountered several stops and detours on his journey, such as the pit, Potiphar's house, and prison. At times, he thought his dreams were dying, but purpose and destiny brought him to the palace.

Let me emphasize again that God is a fixed Principle. Do not allow impatience to deter you from achieving your dream. God works in His own timing, so relinquish your power and right to push, rush, or force Him to do what you want Him to do, when you want Him to do it. Do not be swayed or discouraged. Continue to wait because you could be on the verge of getting the answer that you have been waiting for.

Do not act on impulse. You have been waiting a while. Wait a little while longer. Be determined to keep your focus on His goals for you—like a camera—whatever you focus on, will develop. Trust God even when you are pressured, frustrated, or encumbered with countless questions about how, when, where, and why. Even though you might have tear-filled eyes and feel like enough has become too much, hold on because it will be well worth the wait.

There was a point in time when David, the Psalmist, had a challenge. The Bible declares that he was distressed. He had cause to be overcome with emotion, and as a result, he found consolation as he penned the *Psalm 61* prayer, "Hear my cry, Oh God; attend unto my prayer. From the end of the earth will I cry unto thee, when my heart is overwhelmed; lead me to the rock that is higher than I." Trust God and believe that He is able to help you to overcome your frustration.

Sometimes, while you are waiting for your expected end, life appears calm, and suddenly, a boisterous, windy storm (euroclydon), arises on the ocean of your life, and things become topsy turvy. The tempest begins to rage, billows begin to toss high, but remember that God is right there. You might feel as though He is sleeping but be assured, He is on board. You might have to wake Him up like the disciples did, but you will not perish because He cares, and at any minute, He will take command. Don't lose hope. Your breakthrough is just around the corner. Why would you give up now after you have been waiting so long?

Other situations can also show up in your life as you have purposed in your heart to wait. Wait, no matter what. For example, your long-lasting marriage is now on the rocks, children's behavior and grades in school are unacceptable, the obedient child no longer listens or follows instructions, your workplace is exhibiting the characteristics of a marketplace with insecurity speaking loudly and chaotic, and your adorable pet pooch now barks contentiously and ferociously. Such situations are meant to disrupt and abort the waiting period.

Listen, this is not the time for you to run away from your challenges. Stand your ground and call on the all-seeing, all-knowing, and omnipresent God. Praise Him in the midst of your adversities because what was intended to unearth or uproot you, will stabilize you and work out for your good. Take courage in knowing that God is the captain. He is still onboard the ship of your life. He will speak to your circumstances and tell you when to drop your anchor. So, do not throw away your tackling or your confidence, which carries a great recompense of reward. Just know that your anchor holds, though your ship may be battered. Your anchor holds, though your sails are torn. *Know also that you have an anchor that keeps the soul steadfast and sure while the billows roll. It is fastened to the rock, which cannot move, and is grounded firm and deep in the Savior's love.*[6]

The impotent man had waited at the Pool of Bethesda for thirty-eight years. He had an encounter with Jesus, who asked him if he wanted to be made whole. His answer was neither negative nor positive. He told the Lord that every year, at a certain time, an angel would come down and disturb the water, and he had no one to help to put him in the pool. Sometimes our progress can be delayed by our responses and our dependence on others. This man—who was playing the blame game—was able to master what had mastered him for so long. He was relieved of his infirmity by the Healer Divine.

Regardless of how long it takes to get your answer or breakthrough, I encourage you to be direct and specific about your situation. Wait on the Lord: be of good courage, and He shall strengthen your heart: wait, I say on the Lord *(Psalm 27:14)*. The psalmist David said, "I waited patiently on the Lord, and He inclined unto me, and He heard my cry," *(Psalm 40:1)*.

Continue to wait on the Lord, and in the end you will be overjoyed that you are victorious after what seemed to be a never-ending wait.

Chapter Nine

Faith While You Wait

What is faith?

Now faith is the assurance (title deed, confirmation) of things hoped for (divinely guaranteed), and the evidence of the things not seen (the conviction of their reality). Faith comprehends as fact what cannot be experienced by the physical senses. *(Hebrews 11:1).*

Faith is believing what God says. It is the prerequisite to receiving anything from the Lord. In other words, it is a thing that is required as a precondition for something else to happen or exist.

It is stated in *Mark 11:24,* "Therefore, I say unto you whatsoever things you desire, when you pray, you must believe that you receive, and you shall have everything that God has given to you in Christ." When God places His imprint on your heart or mind, He wants you to believe what He says, appropriate and take it. He wants you to act on what He said. He told Joshua that every place that the soles of his feet tread upon, was his for the taking. Yet, Joshua refused to step out and walk all over the real estate and claim what God had for him. Claim what God has for you! It's yours. Walk it out and let God work it out.

A person who doubts, waivers, or asks amiss will not receive anything from the Lord. You need solid faith and tenacious faith to receive anything from the Lord. *James 1:7-9* declares, "Let not that man think that he shall receive anything from the Lord. A double-minded person is unstable in all his ways."

Sometimes, as we wait on God, we sit idly doing nothing. Let us strike up a chord of worship and praise. These are two catalysts that can thrust us right into our destiny. Paul and Silas sang praises while they were in jail, and their praises sped up their victory and release. While the children of Israel were going to battle, they also sang praises to the Lord, which also helped to seal their victory.

Satan and his emissaries are adamant about preventing God's people from receiving what He has for us, but the Word tells us to FEAR NOT! Faith is the opposite of fear. Fear and faith do not go together. They are not bedfellows, and there is no compatibility between the two. Because a person declares they have faith, that does not mean they are off the hook, or the devil is not monitoring them. Satan is like a roaring lion— going to and fro, seeking whom he may devour. Remember what he did to Job. Consider Job's losses, yet he still said, "All my appointed time, I will wait until my change comes." His time came with twice as many blessings.

As you wait, continue to read God's Word, fast, and pray. Do not sit in the seat of complacency any longer, that is not what faith is. Faith is our constant dependence on the One who has the last word, who has the answer to our waiting.

If there is any consolation, remember this: Lazarus was already dead. Mary and Martha sent for his friend Jesus, who took four days to get to their house in Bethany. These two sisters did not exercise faith when Jesus arrived. Recall their outbursts: "You are my brother's friend, he died, and we have sent for you. Where were you? Where have you been, and what took you so long?" Martha exclaimed.

"I blame you, Jesus!" said Mary, "If you were here, and if you did not take so long to come, my brother, Lazarus, would still be alive! It has been four days, and his body stinks!"

Sometimes, you can be at the brink of a breakthrough, yet a further delay arises. Remember that delay is not denial. Sometimes, circumstances change or worsen while we are waiting. But we still cannot afford to give up. I know that it gets frustrating, but stop giving in to your frustrations because doing that will not make things any better. Be patient and trust God.

Remember, God is a fixed Principle. He will not work on your time, but He will be on time. He walks and operates in resurrection power. He told Mary and Martha, "Your brother is not dead, he is sleeping, and he will wake up."

Mary replied, "Not now, you are talking about the resurrection." She still exhibited a lack of faith and did not understand God's timing. According to *Psalms 89:34,* God declares He will not break the covenant He has established, nor will He alter the things which has gone out of His lips.

What things? Jesus said, "I am the resurrection and the life, the one who believes in Me will live even though they die. And whoever lives by believing in Me, will never die. Do you believe this? Did I not tell you that if you believe you will see the glory of God."

After the sisters showed some faith, Jesus said, "Show me where they laid him. Blessed are they who believe before they see." He commanded them to roll away the stone, then He called Lazarus, "Lazarus come forth!" Lazarus came forth, still bound in his grave clothes. "Loose him and let him go," commanded Jesus. They did as He instructed. *(John 39-40)*.

Regardless of what tries to deter you while you are waiting, or the length of your wait, know that Jesus is on His way. Even though He tarries, wait for Him, and wait on Him. Whatever He promised, no one else has the power to affect or change your situation like Him. He has no predecessor, and He has no successor. He is all power and all life. Reach out to Him as He reaches out to you. If the Word of God requires faith, then faith must be activated. So then, activate your faith, then exercise it as you wait.

CHAPTER Ten

Now Activate Your Faith

Faith is the cornerstone or foundation on which our trust must be built. Faith cannot be built on fear, impatience, denial or frustration. It requires devotion, determination, and a made-up mind.

The word of God requires faith for one to realize their goal, therefore, then faith must be released or activated. Faith must be activated with the receiver's involvement, participation, and tenacity.

Blind Bartimaeus heard that Jesus was passing his way, so he cried out "Jesus, thou Son of David, have mercy on me," as he hoped to receive his sight.

He was ridiculed and harassed by the crowd as he was told to shut up. The Bible declared that he cried out the more, and with such tenacity he received his sight.

In Mark 3:1-6, Jesus asked the man with the withered right hand if he wanted to be made well; He responded, and Jesus told him to stretch forth his right hand which he did. That was a stretch of faith which resulted in his healing.

Activating our faith happens when God's word speaks to our hearts, we choose to believe it, then we act in ways which line up with what we say we believe. Not in a way that coerces God to act on our behalf, but in a way that says we trust God is working, no matter what.[7]

How to Activate Your Faith:
1. Be Determined
2. Be Focused
3. Remove Doubt and Unbelief
4. Pray
5. Fast
6. Worship
7. Praise
8. Stand on the promises of God

References

[1] George Eastman. (2020). Retrieved from
https://www.biography.com/inventors/george-eastman

[2] https://discoverpoetry.com/poems/william-edward-hickson/try-again/

[3] Dr. Seuss Biography. Retrieved from
https://www.thefamouspeople.com/profiles/theodor-geisel-3757.php

[4] https://web.archive.org/web/20051225125934/http://www.publ ishersweekly.com/article/CA186995.html

[4b] https://www.theguardian.com/books/2019/jan/30/thank-you-letter-to-man-who-saved-the-cat-in-the-hat

[5] ElChriscoButter. (2011). George Banton If You Stumble And Fall [Video]. YouTube. https://www.youtube.com/watch?v=-QADOQXujiI

[6] Official Viv Iris. (2020). Will your anchor hold (Afro beat Rendition) by Viv Iris [Video]. YouTube.
https://www.youtube.com/watch?v=ebb-hCnbo08

[7] https://jolenunderwood.com/choose-activated-faith

The End

www.ingramcontent.com/pod-product-compliance
Lightning Source LLC
Chambersburg PA
CBHW060352130626
46553CB00003B/1196